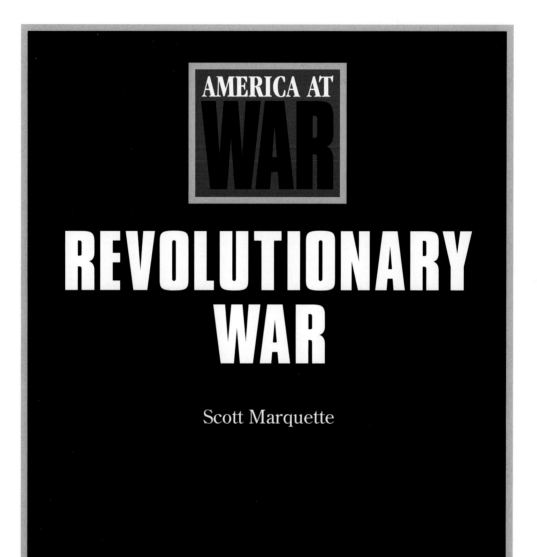

AMERICA AT WAR

REVOLUTIONARY WAR

Scott Marquette

Rourke Publishing LLC
Vero Beach, Florida 32964

Rourke
Publishing LLC

PHOTO CREDITS:
Marine Corps Art Collection: cover, pages 8, 24; U.S. Army Center of Military History: pages 4, 6, 14, 16, 23, 32, 33, 35, 40; Defense Visual Information Center: pages 10, 12, 15, 18, 20, 21, 26, 28, 30, 36, 38, 44; National Archives and Records Administration, page 42.

PRODUCED by Lownik Communication Services, Inc. www.lcs-impact.com
DESIGNED by Cunningham Design

Library of Congress Cataloging-in-Publication Data

Marquette, Scott.
  Revolutionary War / Scott Marquette.
      p. cm. — (America at war)
  Summary: Traces the events of the American Revolution, from the early protests such as the Boston Tea Party through the election of George Washington as President in 1789.
Includes bibliographical references and index.
  ISBN 1-58952-387-3 (hardcover)
  1. United States—History—Revolution, 1775-1783—Juvenile literature.
[1. United States—History—Revolution, 1775-1783.] I. Title. II.
America at war (Rourke Publishing)

E208 .M347 2002
973.3—dc21   2002001241

Printed in the USA

Cover Image:
General George Washington orders his troops to attack Hessian soldiers at Princeton on January 3, 1777.

Table of Contents

Farmers and woodsmen
faced the mighty British army during
the American Revolution.

A Nation Is Born

More than two hundred years ago, an amazing thing happened. Farmers started a war with the greatest army on Earth. It was the war that created our country.

They fought to form a new nation. They fought for the ideals of liberty and freedom. The first shot fired in that battle was called "The Shot Heard Round the World." Its echoes still ring today.

The colonists won their fight to be free from Britain. Their war made history. For the first time, a **colony** made itself free. The nation they built was the first to let people choose their leaders.

They called their nation the United States of America. It became the strongest country in history. Today, their victory still inspires Americans and people around the world.

Even though the Americans had smaller armies and fewer weapons, they held on to win their freedom from Britain.

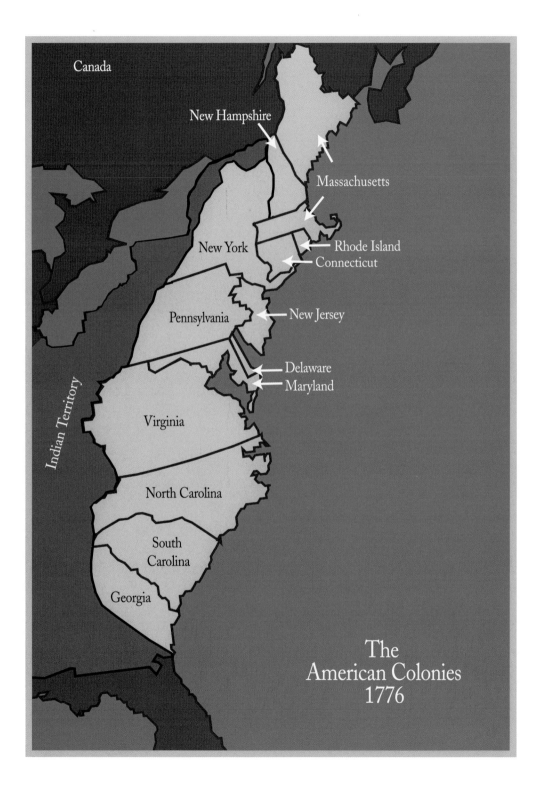

The American Colonies 1776

REVOLUTIONARY WAR TIMELINE

1607
First British colony in America

1756–1763
The Seven Years' War

1765
Britain imposes new taxes on the colonies

1770
March 5: The Boston Massacre

1773
December 16: The Boston Tea Party

1775
April 9: Minutemen fire on British troops at Lexington

1776
July 4: Declaration of Independence signed

August: Battle of New York

December 26: Washington crosses the Delaware to defeat British at Trenton

1777
October: Battle of Saratoga

1777–1778
Winter at Valley Forge

1778
February: French join with Americans

1781
October 19: British surrender at Yorktown

1783
November 30: Treaty of Paris signed

1787
September 19: Constitution ratified

The Colonies Revolt

The first people who came from Europe to the New World lived in colonies. Colonies were large areas of land ruled by the nations of Europe. In time, Britain ruled thirteen colonies in America.

But Britain was very far away. It took weeks to cross the Atlantic Ocean by ship. It was hard to send people or messages back and forth. That made the colonists feel that they could run their own lives. They had their own leaders and made their own laws.

At first, Britain let the colonists do as they pleased. Britain wanted to buy the crops the colonies grew. It also wanted to sell goods to the colonists. But in the 1700s, things changed.

Britain began to fight with France over control of the New World. The **Seven Years' War** lasted from

King George III

King George III ruled Britain from 1760 to 1820. He spent most of his long reign fighting with France. He was not a very able king, but he was very stubborn. By 1811 he was blind and insane.

Crispus Attucks, an escaped slave,
was one of the first victims of British gunfire in
the Boston Massacre.

1756 to 1763. When it ended, Britain ruled the eastern half of America.

The war had cost Britain great sums of money. Britain wanted the colonies to share more of the cost. It put new taxes on goods the colonists bought.

The new taxes made many colonists angry. They had no say in the laws Britain made. They said the new laws were **"taxation without representation."** Some said the colonies should be free from Britain. They were called **patriots**.

A riot broke out in Boston in 1770. British troops shot at an angry mob. Crispus Attucks, an escaped slave, was the first of many killed. The riot was known as "The Boston Massacre." It fueled the desire of patriots to be free.

In 1772, Britain put a tax on tea. In Boston, some men decided to protest. They dressed up as Native Americans. Then they threw all the tea from the ships into Boston Harbor. "The Boston Tea Party" made Britain even stricter with the colonies.

Leaders from each colony came to Philadelphia in 1774. They met to discuss what to do about the trouble with Britain. This was the first **Continental Congress**. The Congress did not agree to break with the crown. But it sent a protest to the king. The Congress decided to get ready for war.

*Minutemen fire on British troops at the
Battle of Lexington. The first shot was called
"The Shot Heard Round the World."*

The war clouds gathered. In April 1775, the English king sent troops to capture patriot leaders. Paul Revere rode to warn people about the raid. Patriots called **minutemen** fired on the English troops in Lexington, Massachusetts. They were the first shots of the American Revolution.

A group of Massachusetts militiamen stand their ground against a uniformed line of British soldiers.

A Tiny Army Clings to Hope

The armies of Britain and the colonies were very different. When the war began, Britain had the most powerful army in the world. Its soldiers were well trained and well fed. They wore fine uniforms. The officers had a great deal of experience. Some of the soldiers were not English. Some were from countries like Germany. They fought for pay.

Most men who fought the British were farmers and woodsmen with little experience of war.

Most of the patriots had never fought before. Few of them had uniforms. They fought with the rifles they used for hunting. Usually there was no money to pay them. Often they had to go without food. But they fought to make their country free. That made them loyal and brave.

15

The British charge the patriot trenches during the Battle of Bunker Hill.

The British troops fought in long rows called ranks. When they fired their **muskets** in ranks, the effect was deadly. Colonists would sometimes fight from behind trees and rocks or use sneak attacks. This way they could make the best use of a small force.

The colonists showed their power at the Battle of Bunker Hill near Concord, Massachusetts. After fighting with the patriots in April, the British army fell back on the town of Concord. The colonists dug trenches in the hills above town. On June 17, 1775, the British army marched up the hill to drive the colonists out.

The colonists waited until the enemy was close. Then they fired from their trenches. They drove the British back. The British charged again. Again, the colonists drove them back. On the third try, the British finally took the hill. But by then they had lost 1,000 men. The colonists lost the battle. But they showed they could hold their own against the British.

The next summer, the Continental Congress met again. They agreed to break with Britain. On July 4, 1776, they signed the **Declaration of Independence**. It said that all men

The Farmer-Soldiers of the Revolution

Many of the American soldiers were farmers. Often they would fight for a short time, then return home to work their farms. They lacked experience. But they knew the countryside better than the British.

Benjamin Franklin (standing, left),
Thomas Jefferson (seated, holding paper),
and John Adams (standing, right)
were among the leaders who wrote the
Declaration of Independence.

were equal and had the right to choose their own government. The former colonies were now the United States of America. The Congress also chose George Washington to lead the army.

That summer, Washington built up an army of 20,000 troops in New York. The British sent an army of 32,000 to meet them. On August 27, 1776, the British attacked. Washington's men fought hard. But the large enemy army was too strong. The American army was pushed out of New York and had to retreat to New Jersey. It was a terrible defeat for Washington.

On Christmas night, 1776, General Washington moved his troops across the Delaware River for a surprise attack on Hessian soldiers.

Victory, Then Defeat

After the defeats in New York and New Jersey, Washington's army was in trouble. Morale was low. People wondered if the British could really be beaten. France was watching to see if it should help the Americans. Washington knew he had to win a victory.

He devised a daring plan. German soldiers, called **Hessians**, were fighting for the British. They were camped in Trenton, New Jersey. Washington knew the Hessians would enjoy a big party at Christmas. He bet that they would let down their guard.

On Christmas night 1776, Washington went on the attack. His army crossed the Delaware River. Boats carried men, horses, and guns. It took them all night to cross. Early the next day, the Americans

The patriot soldiers, many dressed only in rags, suffered through the bitter winter at Valley Forge.

The Continental Congress

The Continental Congress was the first U.S. government. It was made up of representatives of the thirteen colonies. It met in Philadelphia. Such great leaders as John Adams, Benjamin Franklin, and Thomas Jefferson served on the Congress.

attacked the sleeping Hessians. Washington's plan worked. The British commander was killed. More than 1,000 Hessians were taken prisoner. It was a major victory.

A few days later, Washington attacked the British again. He met them at Princeton, New Jersey. This time, the British were much stronger. But the British general, Charles Cornwallis, split up his troops. Washington attacked half his army. It was another win for the Americans.

The two victories gave the patriot cause hope. Washington showed that he could beat the British. Congress tried to raise more troops and money for Washington's army.

But the Americans' luck did not last. In September 1777, the British General William Howe decided to capture the American capital, which was then in Philadelphia. Washington tried to block him at Brandywine Creek. But Howe was able to trick

*When General Washington
attacked the Hessians in Trenton at dawn,
he found them unprepared.*

Washington. Soon, the American army was
surrounded. Washington's troops had to escape in
the night. They could not defend Philadelphia.

Howe was able to take the American capital without
firing a shot. The Congress had to flee. A few days
later, Washington was again beaten, this time at

*Washington won another victory
by attacking British General Cornwallis's
troops in Princeton, New Jersey.*

Germantown. In defeat, his troops fled to Valley Forge for the winter.

That winter was the worst time of the entire war. There was much snow and bitter cold. Troops lived in huts made from sticks. There was little food and no money. Winter clothes and shoes were scarce. Men wrapped their feet in rags. Many died. Troops began to run away from the army. Many thought the patriots would have to give up their dream of freedom.

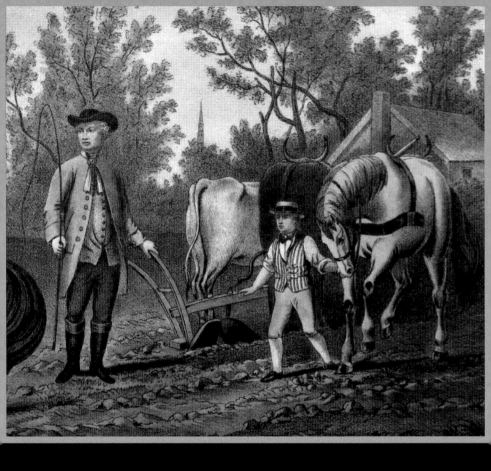

*Many Americans
lived on farms in 1776 and heard little
news of the Revolution.*

The Revolution at Home

If you were an American during the **Revolution**, how would the war affect you? In fact, you might not even be aware of it.

Most Americans lived on farms. They grew or raised their own food. They made nearly everything they used. Men, women, and children all worked very hard. Farm families might live many miles from a town. Many children did not go to school. The only time they might see a neighbor was once a week at church.

When farmers did need to get to town, they traveled by horse or boat. Transportation was slow. It might take them days to get to the nearest town. It was a trip they might make only once or twice a year. As a result, many people did not have the chance to hear news about faraway events.

There was no mass communication. News traveled from town to town by word of mouth. Often, mail carriers on horseback would share the news they had heard. Large towns and cities had newspapers. But the stories in them could be months old. Besides, in most colonies only half

Colonists who lived in cities
got news of the war from town criers
or from large public meetings.

the adults could read. For most Americans, the war must have seemed very remote.

However, for the few Americans who lived in cities, things were different. Town criers would walk the streets, shouting the "headlines." People gathered in taverns and churches to talk about the latest news. And in some cities, people saw the war up close.

In the Battle of New York, the British and American troops fought in the streets of Manhattan. British troops **occupied** New York, Philadelphia, and other American cities. They might force citizens to turn over their homes to the troops. Marching British armies might steal animals and crops to feed themselves.

The Loyalists

Not everyone who lived in the colonies wanted to break with the crown. About one in three people remained loyal to the king. They were called "Loyalists." After the war, many Loyalists moved to Canada.

The men who went to war were sorely missed. On farms, men planted crops, built and repaired fences, and butchered cattle and hogs. When they left, the women and children did as much of this work as they could. But the war made a hard life even harder.

Many women fought alongside men
during the Revolutionary War.

In depictions of the war, we often see only white men. But women and African Americans played a role, too. Women made uniforms, helped feed troops, and served as nurses. A few spied on the British. Some even dressed as soldiers and fought. Most African Americans were slave laborers on farms. But a few fought with the **Continental Army** and some served as spies.

*American soldiers
broke through the British lines at Saratoga,
forcing thousands to surrender.*

Victory for the Revolution

The Americans had one big victory late in 1777. The British invaded the Mohawk Valley in New York state. They wanted to divide the American army in the north from the troops in the south. But the Americans broke through the British lines. They forced nearly 6,000 British troops to surrender at Saratoga. A British plan to split the troops was stopped.

The victory at Saratoga convinced the French to aid the American cause. France

Many American soldiers used long rifles like these. They were more accurate than the muskets the British used.

wanted to hurt Britain. It did not want the Americans to fail. France sent officers, ships, supplies, and some troops. Other Europeans also came to help the Americans. They trained American troops and served as leaders. The aid from across the sea helped keep the patriot cause alive.

The war went on for two more years. There were no major victories on either side. Then, in 1780, the tide began to turn. The Americans won victories in Virginia and North Carolina. The army used **hit-and-run** tactics. They attacked in small, fast groups. Little by little, they wore the British down. Even the battles they lost cost many British lives. The stage was set for the war's end.

In April 1781, the British army tried and failed to trap an American force in Virginia. But more American troops arrived. Cornwallis feared his army would be trapped instead. He moved his army to the sea to be close to the British fleet.

Washington saw his chance. Swiftly, he moved his troops in from the north. French troops moved in from the south. To keep from alerting the British, the armies had to march hundreds of miles in a few

Rifles Vs. Muskets

One thing in favor of the Americans was the guns they used. They used rifles, like the Kentucky Long Rifle. Rifles had long barrels and could fire more accurately than the shorter muskets the British used. With rifles, Americans could shoot British troops before they were in musket range.

weeks. More than 17,000 American forces faced 6,000 British troops. At the same time, French ships moved in off the coast. By September, Cornwallis was trapped at Yorktown. A fleet of British ships tried to rescue him but failed.

In the end, Washington captured the British troops without firing a shot. The British

Colonial troops won many victories against British troops in Virginia and North Carolina, using hit-and-run tactics.

In October 1781,
General Cornwallis was trapped at Yorktown. He was
forced to surrender to General Washington.

surrendered on October 19, 1781. As the captured troops marched away, the band played "The World Turned Upside Down."

The next year, the British and Americans signed a peace treaty in Paris. The former British colonies now belonged to the United States of America. A new nation was born.

George Washington was a national hero by the end of the Revolution. He became the country's first president.

"We the People"

The former colonies had won their freedom from Britain. Now came the tough job: to start a country of their own.

During the war, the Continental Congress had drawn up a plan for the new nation. It was called **"The Articles of Confederation."** Under this plan, the states were only loosely tied together. The central government was weak. It could ask the states for money, but it could not tax. It could not pass laws that went against state laws. This weak system caused many problems during the war. The country's leaders knew they would need a better plan. In 1785, they began drafting a new **constitution**.

There was much argument about how the new government should be formed. After all, the leaders

George Washington

George Washington was the son of a wealthy farmer. He became a surveyor and later served in the Seven Years' War. After the Revolution, some people wanted to make him king. But after two terms as president, he retired to his farm, Mount Vernon.

*George Washington awarded
special medals to those who had served
with honor in the Revolutionary War.*

had no model to go by. At last, they agreed on a system that shared power among three branches: Congress, the courts, and the president. The central government was stronger. But it still shared power with the states. Above all, it was based on the will of the people. The Constitution was adopted in 1788.

George Washington was elected the nation's first president in 1789. He was much loved as a hero of the war. He could have made himself very powerful. But Washington always acted as a servant of the people. He served just two terms. His actions were the model for all the presidents to come.

In the years after the war, the new nation came into its own. More people began settling the vast lands in the west. Political parties were formed. The kind of **democracy** we know today emerged. In the new nation, women could not vote. People still owned slaves. It took many years for the ideals of freedom to be realized.

Today, our nation still tries to live by the ideals the patriots fought for. We believe that the power of government comes from the people. And we believe every person has rights no one can take away. We still argue about the best way for government to work. But we solve our disputes through our elected officials.

After the war, the Congress
created a Constitution to describe
a new system of government.

The story of how farmers fought to be free has inspired people around the world. Today, many nations are building new democracies, just as Americans did more than 200 years ago.

The ideals that moved the original patriots still inspire people around the world today.

Further Reading

Bliven, Bruce. *The American Revolution*. Random House, 1987.

Hakim, Joy. *From Colonies to Country*. Oxford University Press, 1999.

McGovern, Ann. *The Secret Soldier: The Story of Deborah Sampson*. Scholastic, 1999.

Moore, Kay. *If You Lived at the Time of the American Revolution*. Scholastic, 1998.

Murphy, Jim. *A Young Patriot: The American Revolution As Experienced by One Boy*. Houghton Mifflin, 1998.

Websites to Visit
The American Revolution: National Discussion of Our Revolutionary Origins www.revolution.h-net.msu.edu

LIBERTY! The American Revolution
www.pbs.org/ktca/liberty/

Glossary

Articles of Confederation — the first plan for the American government

colony — a settlement ruled by a foreign nation

constitution — a document that sets the rules for a government

Continental Army — the regular troops raised by Congress to fight the British

Continental Congress — leaders from the thirteen colonies who formed the first United States government

Declaration of Independence — document that declared the colonies a new nation, free from Britain

democracy — form of government in which leaders are elected by the people

Hessians — German soldiers who were paid to fight for the British

hit-and-run — fighting that uses quick sneak attacks

Loyalists — colonists who supported the British

minutemen — patriots who pledged to be ready to fight the British at a minute's notice

muskets — guns used by British troops; they were deadly, but not very accurate

occupied — taken over by an army

patriots — colonists who thought Americans should be free from Britain

representatives — leaders elected by the people to serve in the government

revolution — a great change in government or society, often through violence

Seven Years' War — war between France and Britain over control of America

taxation without representation — forcing people to pay taxes when they have no elected representatives in the government

Index